I0384652

STAR WARS™

TIE FIGHTER

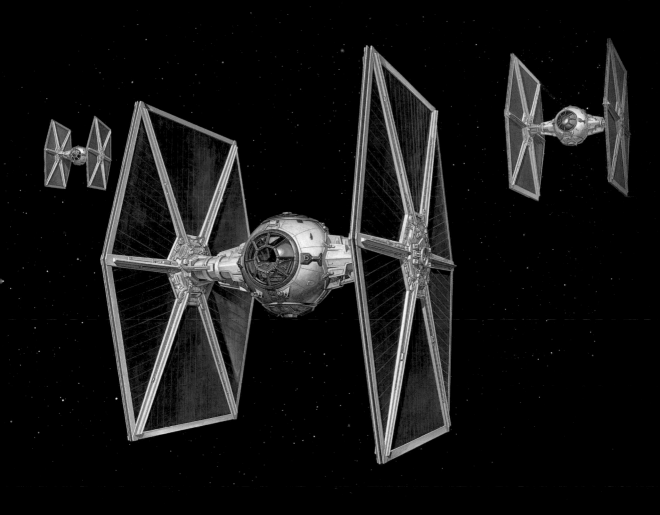

STAR WARS

TIE FIGHTER

INSIDE THE EMPIRE'S WINGED MENACE

WRITTEN BY MICHAEL KOGGE

INCREDI BUILDS

A Division of Insight Editions, LP
San Rafael, California

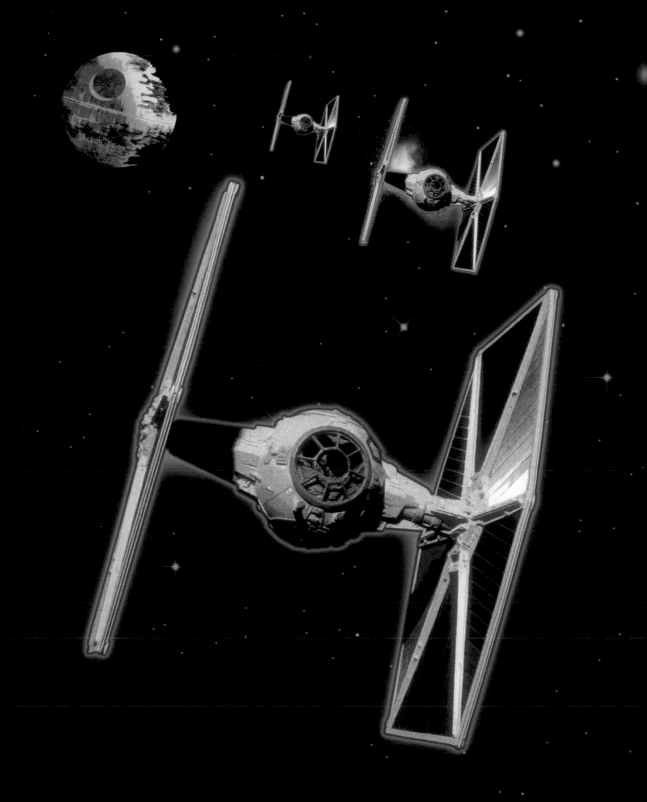

INTRODUCTION

IF STORMTROOPERS ARE the face of the Galactic Empire on the ground, TIE fighters are their equivalent in air and space. They bear the simplest of designs—two solar energy–collecting wings connected to a cockpit ball with twin ion engines—and have the simplest of purposes: vanquish the enemy using overwhelming numbers. For wherever there is one TIE, there must be another—and another, and another. These swift and spry starfighters swarm their quarry like flies around a bantha, buzzing and blasting their way to victory. Starship captains know that, once chased, it's almost better to surrender. Even if you evade or destroy a TIE, there are usually three more to take its place.

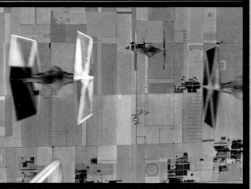

Fear is perhaps the most powerful weapon in a TIE's arsenal. From the scream of its engines to the way its cockpit viewport resembles an Imperial crest, every aspect of the TIE fighter is intended to menace and terrify. The Emperor is said to gloat over reports of how patrols of approaching TIEs send Rebel combatants running for their lives. Darth Vader himself flies a TIE fighter, modified for his purposes with its inclined wings and devastating laser cannons. Yet perhaps the most formidable attribute of any TIE fighter is its pilot, who is guaranteed to be highly trained and capable of doing feats in a TIE unimaginable in any other craft. And since the standard TIEs don't have the luxury of a hyperdrive, one can be assured that pilots won't quit until their mission is completed or their TIE (and their life) is no longer.

The number of TIE fighters only continues to increase. As the Empire expands its dominion over the galaxy, thousands of TIEs come out of the factories of Sienar Fleet Systems every standard year. While minor updates have been made and some specialized craft have been produced, the basic structure of the TIE fighter has remained the same since its first assembly. This conformity of design not only improves the ease of replacement but also its deployment in battle. All naval officers from pilots to admirals know the TIE's exact capabilities and can strategize how to most effectively utilize the fighter for specific missions. Ever since the waning years of the Republic, it would be hard to pinpoint another military starship that has lasted as long or has made as much impact as the TIE fighter.

TIE FIGHTER

The TIE/ln is the base model of the Imperial fighter and has been manufactured in the largest quantities. Small but swift, these agile starships are found wherever the Empire is.

TECHNICAL SPECIFICATIONS

MANUFACTURER: Sienar Fleet Systems

MODEL: TIE/ln

CLASS: Starfighter

LENGTH/WIDTH/HEIGHT: 8.9 m x 10.71 m x 9.125 m

WEAPONRY: Two forward-mounted laser cannons

SHIELDS: None

MAXIMUM SPEED: 4,100 G (space) / 1,200 kph (atmosphere)

HYPERDRIVE: None

LIFE SUPPORT SYSTEMS: Yes

CREW: 1

SUSTENANCE PACKS: Two-day supply

COST: 60,000 Imperial credits new; 25,000 used (military requisition charges)

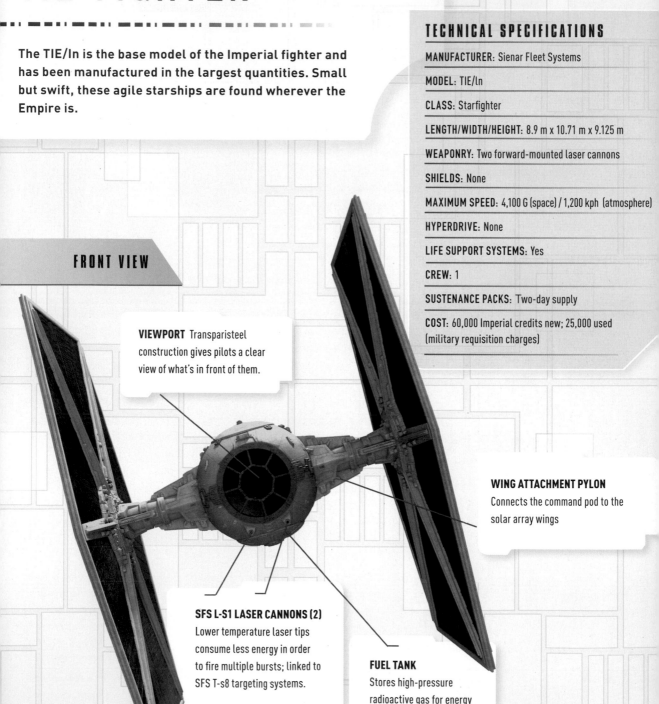

FRONT VIEW

VIEWPORT Transparisteel construction gives pilots a clear view of what's in front of them.

WING ATTACHMENT PYLON
Connects the command pod to the solar array wings

SFS L-S1 LASER CANNONS (2)
Lower temperature laser tips consume less energy in order to fire multiple bursts; linked to SFS T-s8 targeting systems.

FUEL TANK
Stores high-pressure radioactive gas for energy conversion in reactor

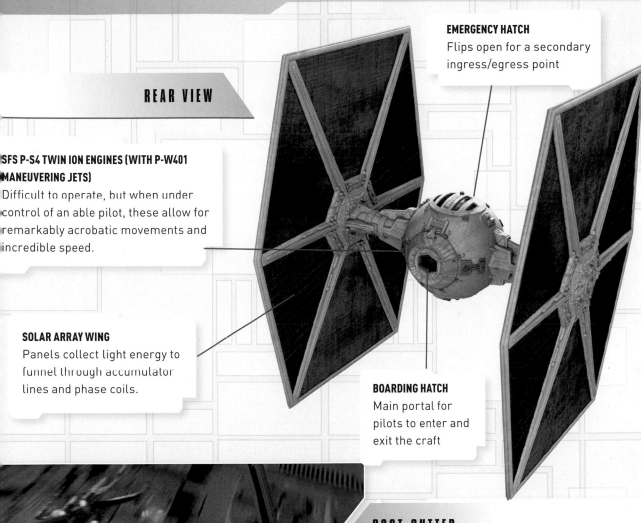

EMERGENCY HATCH
Flips open for a secondary ingress/egress point

SFS P-S4 TWIN ION ENGINES (WITH P-W401 MANEUVERING JETS)
Difficult to operate, but when under control of an able pilot, these allow for remarkably acrobatic movements and incredible speed.

SOLAR ARRAY WING
Panels collect light energy to funnel through accumulator lines and phase coils.

BOARDING HATCH
Main portal for pilots to enter and exit the craft

COST-CUTTER

The secret to the TIE fighter's success is not its speed or armaments—it's its cost. Sienar Fleet Systems designed a starship that could be cheaply replicated with standardized parts and sold to the Imperial Navy in bulk. It furnished the TIE with the essentials—and only the essentials. Some pilots have even remarked that the TIE is nothing but two engines strapped to a seat. But those twin ion engines pack quite a punch, achieving velocities greater than anything else available in the commercial marketplace. It would take one incredibly souped-up star freighter to outrace a TIE.

WORTHY ADVERSARY

Though lacking deflector shields, TIE fighters have the velocity, maneuverability, and laser cannons to deal with enemies of the Empire.

CONNECTED CANNONS

In its initial production phase, the TIE's fire-linked lasers siphoned energy from the ion engines. Later models added a small generator to the belly of the cockpit, which powered the cannons and let the engines be used solely for acceleration and movement.

LOW MAINTENANCE

The TIE is a hallmark of efficient design practices. Its ion engines possess no moving parts, and they break down much less often than X-wings or Y-wings. Those few TIEs that are damaged and need fixing are usually substituted by other TIEs that are fully operational. The Empire has the resources to make quick replacements rather than waste time on difficult repairs!

NO HYPERDRIVE, NO PROBLEM

The lack of a hyperdrive was a design decision that helped make the TIE so cost-effective. TIEs work in unison with larger vessels and are carried through hyperspace either inside a Star Destroyer's hangar or by docking to a Gonzanti assault cruiser's underside. Moreover, this deficiency eliminates the problem of desertion. Pilots with rebellious thoughts can't jump away from a fierce combat zone—they have to fight or die!

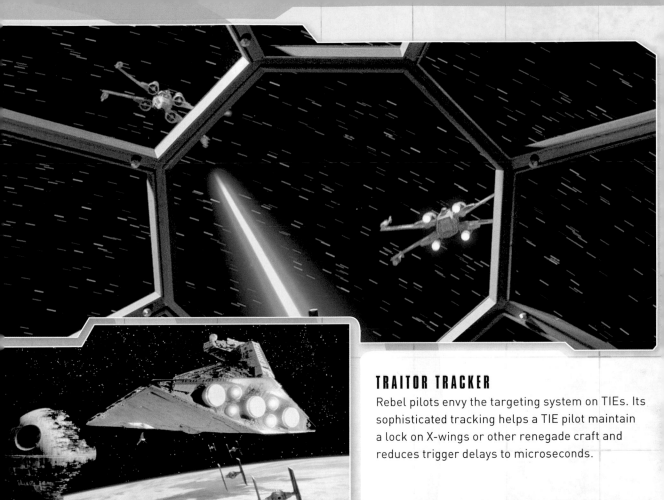

TRAITOR TRACKER

Rebel pilots envy the targeting system on TIEs. Its sophisticated tracking helps a TIE pilot maintain a lock on X-wings or other renegade craft and reduces trigger delays to microseconds.

TIE HIVE

An Imperial Star Destroyer racks an attack wing of TIEs (48 TIE/ln fighters, 12 TIE bombers, and 12 TIE interceptors), while the many hangar decks on the first Death Star can hold 100 squadrons—totaling 7,200 TIEs!

ALL TOGETHER NOW

Although TIEs are sent on solo scout missions, rarely do they fly alone in combat areas because their vulnerabilities make them easy targets. To counteract this, TIEs usually patrol in pairs or groups of four, and an attack squadron numbers twelve fighters. Six squadrons form a full attack wing of seventy-two fighters, which can be an imposing challenge for a single rebel defense squadron!

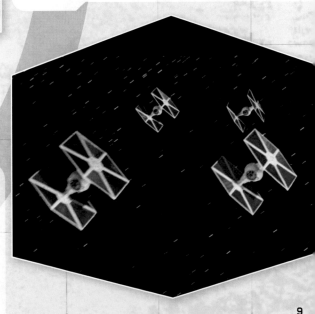

PILOTS

Among the most respected members of the Imperial military establishment, the men and women who fly TIE fighters risk their lives in the unforgiving vacuum of space for the greater glory of the Empire.

ONLY THE BEST

Those desiring to become Imperial pilots must submit to comprehensive physical, psychological, and emotional tests. A mere ten percent of applicants are chosen—and far fewer remain after the intense training. However, during the war against the Rebel Alliance, heavy casualties in the pilot corps opened up the ranks for those who might not have been selected in the past.

ELEPHANT MEN

TIEs possess minimal life support systems and in case of emergency all pilots wear a vac-sealed flight suit with a life support pack attached to their chest. Resembling small elephantine trunks, two gas transfer hoses pump oxygen into the helmet for pilots to breathe. Also invaluable are the positive gravity pressure boots that allow precise control of the TIE's foot yokes.

TEAM PLAYERS

TIE pilots appear arrogant and aloof to their comrades in other branches of the Imperial Navy when in fact, during the heat of battle, there are no better team players. They share a bond with each other that is stronger than the one that exists between other service members. In order to survive a dogfight in their vulnerable ships, TIE pilots have to completely trust that their comrades are watching their backs.

SHOOT FIRST

An enemy's well-placed shot can cripple or destroy a TIE, since it has no shields to deflect fire. Consequently, pilots are schooled in evasion techniques and are taught to fire the TIE's lasers before the enemy can trigger a barrage.

DARTH VADER'S TIE FIGHTER TECHNICAL SPECIFICATIONS

At Darth Vader's request, Sienar Fleet Systems produced a series of advanced TIE fighters that met his personal specifications. Though no faster or maneuverable than the standard TIE, these limited-run prototypes possessed additional weaponry and features that made them far more powerful.

ELITES ONLY

Other than Lord Vader, only select individuals of merit flew the TIE advanced, giving them a reputation as the most dangerous starfighters in the Imperial Navy.

TECHNICAL SPECIFICATIONS

MANUFACTURER: Sienar Fleet Systems

MODEL: TIE Advanced x1 prototype

CLASS: Starfighter

LENGTH/WIDTH/HEIGHT: 11.05 m x 9.35 m x 6.28 m

WEAPONRY: Two forward-mounted laser cannons; cluster missile launcher

SHIELDS: Yes

MAXIMUM SPEED: 4,150 G (space) / 1,200 kph (atmosphere)

HYPERDRIVE: Class 4

LIFE SUPPORT SYSTEMS: Yes

CREW: 1

SUSTENANCE PACKS: Five-day supply

COST: 160,000 Imperial credits new; 65,000 used (military requisition charges)

HYPERDRIVE THERMAL RADIATOR PORTS (AFT)

HIGH-PERFORMANCE SOLAR CELLS

DEFLECTOR SHIELD GENERATOR (IN REAR)

HIGH-POWERED LASER CANNONS

SENSOR ARRAY

INCLINED WING

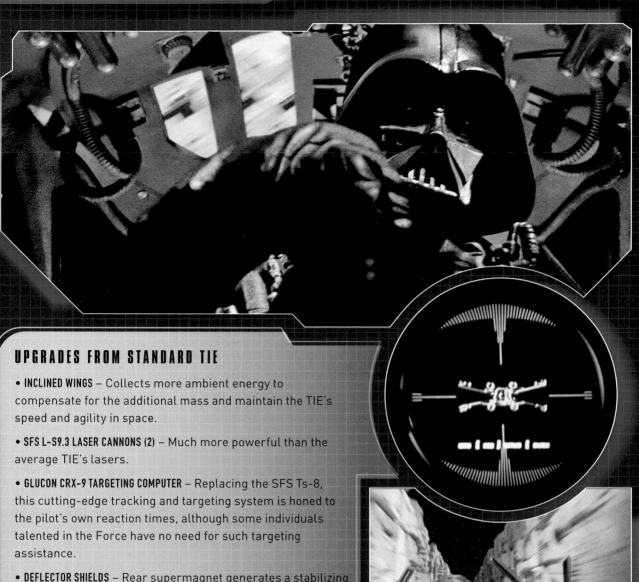

UPGRADES FROM STANDARD TIE

• **INCLINED WINGS** – Collects more ambient energy to compensate for the additional mass and maintain the TIE's speed and agility in space.

• **SFS L-S9.3 LASER CANNONS (2)** – Much more powerful than the average TIE's lasers.

• **GLUCON CRX-9 TARGETING COMPUTER** – Replacing the SFS Ts-8, this cutting-edge tracking and targeting system is honed to the pilot's own reaction times, although some individuals talented in the Force have no need for such targeting assistance.

• **DEFLECTOR SHIELDS** – Rear supermagnet generates a stabilizing field that links projected deflector energies into a shield that surrounds the command pod and wing pylons.

• **SFS P-S5.6 TWIN ION ENGINES** – Boosts energy output needed to carry extra mass and power hyperdrive and deflector shields.

• **HYPERDRIVE** – Class four multiplier with nondroid-assisted navicomputer that stores ten jumps in its memory for quick escapes.

• **REINFORCED HULL** – Extra durasteel plating armor protects against heavy laser barrages.

TIE BOMBER

"Slow but deadly" is an appropriate description for the TIE bomber, because what it lacks in speed, it makes up for in explosive weaponry. Often serving as the Empire's first line of attack, Star Destroyer captains like to send the craft out to carpet bomb large targets like capital ships or ground bunkers and weaken them for the next wave of Imperial forces. The TIE bomber most resembles the TIE advanced except it has two central pods: a starboard cockpit for the pilot and a portside hold for munitions.

TECHNICAL SPECIFICATIONS

MANUFACTURER: Sienar Fleet Systems

MODEL: TIE/sa

CLASS: Light bomber

LENGTH/WIDTH/HEIGHT: 7.9 m x 10.6 m x 5.4 m

WEAPONRY: Two forward-mounted laser cannons; concussion missiles; thermal detonators; proton torpedoes; orbital mines; miscellaneous munitions

SHIELDS: None

MAXIMUM SPEED: 2,380 G (space) / 850 kph (atmosphere)

HYPERDRIVE: None

LIFE SUPPORT SYSTEMS: Yes

CREW: 1

SUSTENANCE PACKS: Two-day supply

COST: 150,000 Imperial credits new; 60,000 used (military requisition charges)

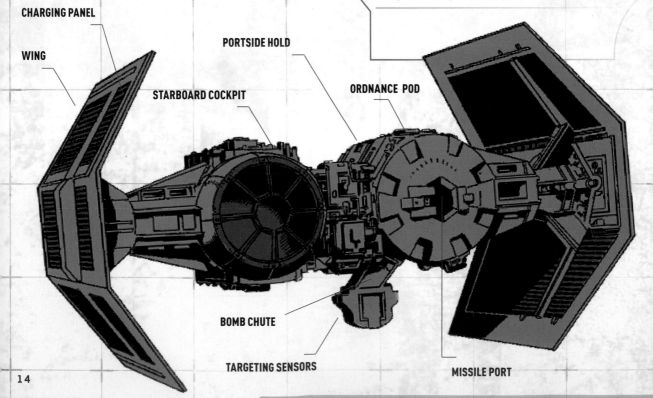

CHARGING PANEL

WING

PORTSIDE HOLD

STARBOARD COCKPIT

ORDNANCE POD

BOMB CHUTE

TARGETING SENSORS

MISSILE PORT

UPGRADES FROM STANDARD TIE

- **INCLINED WINGS** – Design taken from TIE/ad to maximize speed and maneuverability while carrying mass of heavy ordnance.
- **NORDOXICON MICRO INSTRUMENTS' 398X BOMB SIGHT** – Locates surface targets for efficient bombing runs and ordnance drops.
- **SFS T–S7B TARGETING COMPUTER** – Modified for linkage to bomb sight.
- **FORWARD ORDNANCE BAY** – Carries four proton torpedoes or eight concussion missiles.
- **MAIN ORDNANCE BAY** – Carries four proton torpedoes, eight concussion missiles, or eight proton bombs, sixty-four thermal detonators, or six orbital mines. Can also carry stormtroopers.
- **BOMB CHUTE** – Located underneath ordnance pod and connected to targeting sensors.
- **MISSILE PORT** – Located in center of ordnance pod for front-launching of missiles and torpedoes.
- **EJECTOR SEAT** – In case pilots on distant bombing runs need to save themselves.
- **REINFORCED HULL** – Though the bomber lacks shields, quadanium steel alloyed with titanium adds extra protection to ordnance bay and command pod.

BOMBS AWAY!

TIE bombers navigated the dangerous Hoth-Anoat asteroid belt, dropping their ordnance on every rock big enough to be a hiding spot for the *Millennium Falcon*. They never found the *Falcon*, though many Imperial pilots lost their lives in collisions with asteroids.

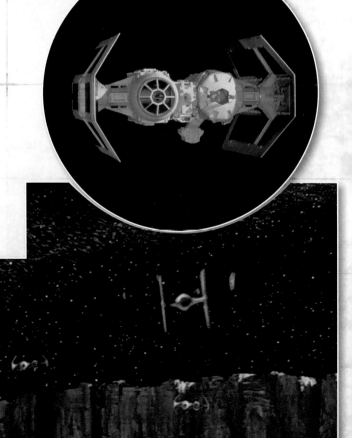

TIE INTERCEPTOR

The fastest and most nimble fighter in the Imperial fleet, the TIE interceptor boasts three times the weaponry of the TIE/ln and offers a much harder target profile for rebel pilots to hit. If one of these interceptors is on your tail, it's almost impossible to shake them off.

TECHNICAL SPECIFICATIONS

MANUFACTURER: Sienar Fleet Systems

MODEL: TIE/in

CLASS: Starfighter

LENGTH/WIDTH/HEIGHT: 11.45 m x 8.08 m x 7.2 m

WEAPONRY: Four wingtip laser cannons; two chin-mounted laser cannons (optional)

SHIELDS: None

MAXIMUM SPEED: 4,240 G (space) / 1250 kph (atmosphere)

HYPERDRIVE: None

LIFE SUPPORT SYSTEMS: Yes

CREW: 1

SUSTENANCE PACKS: Two-day supply

COST: 120,000 Imperial credits new; 50,000 used (military requisition charges)

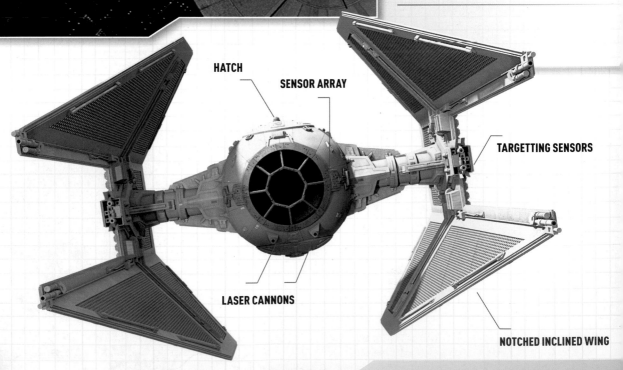

HATCH

SENSOR ARRAY

TARGETTING SENSORS

LASER CANNONS

NOTCHED INCLINED WING

UPGRADES FROM STANDARD TIE

• **NOTCHED INCLINED WINGS** – Carried over from TIE/ad and TIE/sa designs, the ultra-high-efficiency solar arrays on slanted wings absorb more energy for increased speed while central notches above the triangular front panels provide more visibility for pilots.

• **SFS L-S9.3 LASER CANNONS (4)** – Advancements in gas conversion add four more laser cannons with the same energy usage for a total of six cannons: four cannons mounted on front wingtips and two optional cannons that can be mounted under the command pod.

• **SFS T-S9A TARGETING COMPUTER** – Replaces the SFS Ts-8 for more accurate tracking and targeting telemetry.

• **SFS P-S5.6 TWIN ION ENGINES (WITH ION STREAM PROJECTOR)** – Streamlined and standardized from the prototype engines of the TIE advanced, the P-s5.6 twin ion engines permit incredible control over thrust, and the new ion stream projectors enhance a pilot's ability to spin and change direction at a moment's notice.

• **EJECTOR SEAT** – Much requested by pilots, this feature has saved not only lives but also the Imperial funds required for training new pilots.

FIERCE COMPETITION

When the Empire suffered massive losses of TIEs due to the Rebel Alliance's faster A-wing fighter, Sienar Fleet Systems took all the small improvements they had made to TIEs over the years and channeled them into creating a next-generation fighter. The TIE interceptor was born as a result. It nearly matches the A-wing's specs in speed, at a price point that satisfied Imperial bureaucrats.

WING BLASTER CANNON

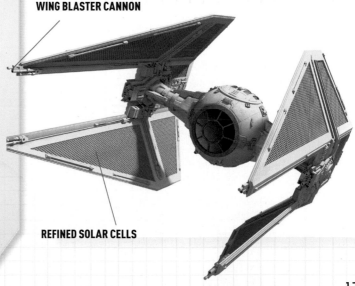

REFINED SOLAR CELLS

THE BATTLE OF YAVIN

TRENCH RUNNERS

The TIEs had a definite advantage navigating the Death Star trench. Three could zip along side-by-side in the narrow lan while only one X-wing or Y-wir could fit in that same space.

Though the first Death Star had thousands of TIEs in its hangars, only a handful were launched to ward off a rebel attack. Those few decimated the rebel squadrons and were but one kill away from ending the Rebel Alliance for good.

GREAT EIGHT

When the vulnerability in the Death Star's reactor was exposed, Darth Vader gathered an elite group of eight TIE pilots to hunt the Rebel fighters down one by one—and nearly succeeded.

NUMBERS GAME

The Rebel Alliance deployed its meager starfighter fleet of only thirty craft, made up of X-wings and Y-wings, against the massive might of the Death Star. Grand Moff Tarkin, believing those starfighters were but an irritant and stood no chance against the Death Star's thousands of turbolaser embankments, did not even dispatch TIE fighters to deal with them.

BYE-BYE BIGGS

Darth Vader eschewed his TIE's targeting computer when he stretched out with the dark side of the Force and blasted apart the X-wing of Luke Skywalker's best friend, Biggs Darklighter.

THE BATTLE OF ENDOR

FLEET VS. FLEET

Thousands of TIE fighters engaged a much smaller but no less substantial number of Alliance craft at Endor. It proved to be one of the biggest, most chaotic dogfights in galactic history.

NO MERCY

When the rebel fleet jumped from hyperspace into the Endor system, the TIE squadrons had already been launched and were ready for battle. One of their primary objectives was to hit the rebels' medical frigate and inflict a blow to rebel morale, forcing them into a defensive position.

SCREAMING SIX

Six TIEs—three TIE/ln fighters and three interceptors—roared after the *Millennium Falcon* and five rebel fighters into the superstructure of the second Death Star. One TIE met a fiery end after skidding off a huge energy conduit. Three others followed the three rebels who broke away from the *Falcon*. The final two interceptors maintained pursuit—and both met their end when the *Falcon*'s lasers blew up the reactor core.

While Han Solo and his rebel strike team worked to disable the half-completed second Death Star's shield, Lando Calrissian and Nien Nunb flew the *Millennium Falcon* through swarms of TIEs above the forest moon of Endor.

IMPERIAL IMPROVEMENTS

By the time of this battle in the *Star Wars* universe, approximately four years after the destruction of the first Death Star, TIE interceptors amounted to about 20 percent of the Imperial fleet.

BEHIND THE SCENES

> *"I came up with 'twin* ion engine fighter.' There were other ideas, like 'Third Intergalactic Empire,' but I thought 'twin-I' engine made more sense."
>
> — *Star Wars* concept artist Joe Johnston

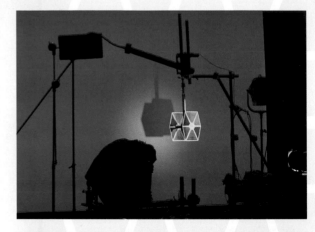

FILMING MINIS

The TIE models were as fragile as they looked. The hot stage lights would often melt and warp their plastic wings during miniature photography!

NO WINDOW

Though Darth Vader was shot inside the same cockpit as the other TIE pilots, keen observers will note that the original model of his TIE Advanced fighter does not have a rear window. It was in the editing phase that filmmaker George Lucas thought that Vader's starfighter should be unique—thus the TIE Advanced was born and a new miniature model was built and shot.

BOOM!

Casting the TIE models in plastic resin made them too difficult to detonate, but less detailed foam models proved better for pyrotechnics work. Model makers could weaken certain areas on the TIE to bear the brunt of the explosion and achieve the desired effect during filming.

DISTINCTIVE ROAR

In a rush to finish audio for a rough cut screening of *Star Wars*, sound designer Ben Burtt threw in random sounds for the TIE fighter engines, even using an elephant shriek for the initial TIE approach to the Death Star. The audience later raved at how amazing the TIEs sounded in that scene, therefore forever tying the sound of a pachyderm to the twin ion engines of the TIEs.

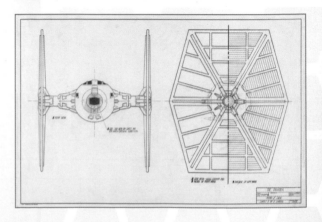

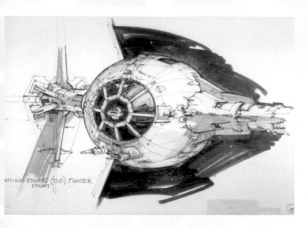

FASCINATING FIRSTS

For the prototype Imperial starfighter, effects veteran Colin Cantwell produced a very simple design without much detail that was essentially a cockpit ball on a stick attached to two square wings. Concept artist Joe Johnston then revised the panel mountings and the glass cockpit window to complete the TIE's famous look.

NEW FOES

Designed by artist Joe Johnston and built by model maker Larry Tan, the TIE interceptor was created to be more terrifying than the original TIE. Its dagger-shaped wings give it a sharper, meaner look, while the orange glow inside the cockpit is reminiscent of fire.

ASSEMBLY LINE

Just as the Empire manufactured large quantities of TIEs, so did the model makers at ILM. They built twenty TIEs to fourteen X-wings!

COLOR SCHEME

In contrast to the battered and bashed-up rebel fighters, the TIEs bore an off-the-conveyer belt, new starship look. Pactra's Stormy Sea Blue became the foundation color for the TIE hull paint jobs, with only a slight weathering effect applied.

BEHIND THE SCENES

LIGHT SHOW

Only four lights were installed on the TIE fighter models: two red lights in the rear and two cannon lights under the front of the cockpit that were used to time the animators' laser streaks.

WORLD WARS

Footage from aerial World War II battles in films such as *Twelve O'Clock High*, *The Dam Busters*, and *The Bridges at Toko-Ri* filled in as crude "animatics" to help the crew visualize the dogfighting between spaceships in the Battle of Yavin. Planes from both the Allies and Axis powers were used interchangeably without regard to rebel or Imperial affiliations.

ARTISTIC INFLUENCE

Referencing Colin Cantwell's models, renowned science fiction painter John Berkey and industrial artist Ralph McQuarrie illustrated the rebel attack on the Death Star. Their vivid work inspired the *Star Wars* filmmakers to imbue the photographed scenes with the same energy.

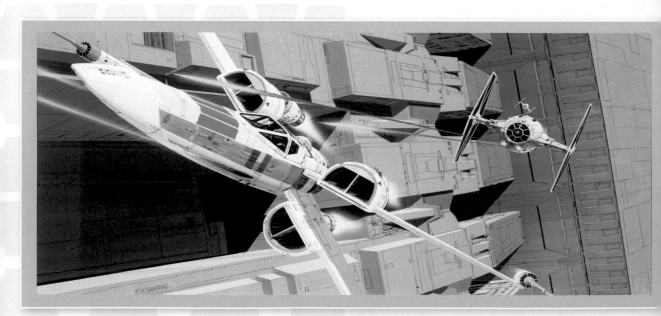

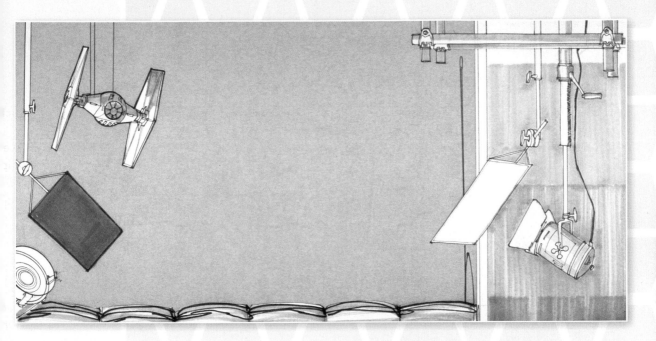

DYKSTRAFLEX

Special photographic effects supervisor John Dykstra developed the first digital motion control camera—dubbed the "Dykstraflex"—to reproduce the precise camera moves and reduce jitter when separately filming various elements like TIEs and X-wings that would later be composited into one shot.

ALWAYS CHANGIN'

For the 1997 Special Edition of *Star Wars*, considerable effort was spent in restoring the dogfight sequence. Computer graphics smoothed out the sometimes jerky movements of the TIEs, which were an artifact of the original motion control photography.

NEVER BEFORE

For *Return of the Jedi*, the nineteenth shot of the Endor space battle labeled "SB 19"—showing the *Millennium Falcon* weaving through hordes of TIEs—was the most complicated special effects sequence ever committed to film at that point. It consisted of sixty-three separate spaceships captured on 170 rolls of film!

TWIN ION BALLET

Choreographing complicated action sequences required editorial assistants to trace onto cellophane the significant movements a TIE made, then stack the cellophane sheets on top of each other to plot out patterns of ships. Attacking TIE squadrons were mapped out in waves of eight.

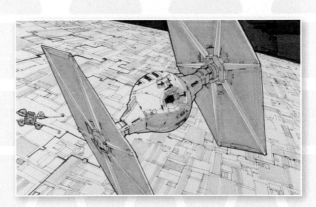

A TIE fighter pilot targets the *Millennium Falcon* in
this Ralph McQuarrie production painting.

DEATH STAR EQUATORIAL CHANNEL

64

A lonely TIE flies above the trenches of the Death Star
in this storyboard from *A New Hope*.

Concept art by Ralph McQuarrie for the original *Star Wars* film shows Colin Cantwell–style prototype TIE fighters approaching a structure that would later inspire Cloud City in *Empire Strikes Back*.

Two TIEs trail the *Millennium Falcon* into the second Death Star's superstructure in this *Return of the Jedi* storyboard.

INTERVIEW WITH THE FATHER OF THE TIE FIGHTER

Cantwell shows Lucas his prototype models in his workshop prior to the beginning of production on *A New Hope*.

Colin Cantwell, a lead member of the special photographic unit for *2001: A Space Odyssey*, was the first artist hired by filmmaker George Lucas during the gestation of *Star Wars*, even before illustrator Ralph McQuarrie. The original models Cantwell had created in his spare time by using parts of various kits convinced Lucas he would be the ideal architect to design the spacecraft of *Star Wars*, among them the X-wing, Star Destroyer, *Millennium Falcon*, and TIE fighter. Cantwell shares his experience for fellow model makers.

HOW DID YOU GET STARTED WORKING WITH GEORGE LUCAS ON THE STARSHIP DESIGNS?

George and I had a story session. I asked him, "What's an important scene?" and "What do you want it to accomplish?" He knew he had to have a Death Star and some kind of a warship. I suggested he also needed a long, skinny ship for the opening.

HOW DID YOU COME UP WITH THE BALL-AND-PERPENDICULAR-WINGS DESIGN OF THE TIE FIGHTER?

The TIE fighter, what's its main characteristic? It's alien. It has something to do with these big sort of solar panels. It's obviously got a cockpit for this evil pilot, but you don't know how he gets in or out. So that was one of the keys to them being sufficiently alien. It also meant for the choreography that it freed up the TIE fighters to have a totally different set of gestures and different non-aerodynamic movements.

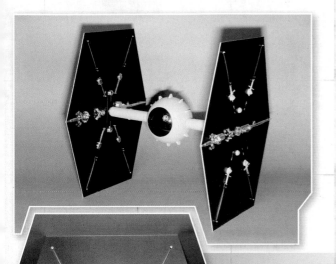

WHAT WERE THE MATERIALS THAT YOU USED TO MAKE YOUR MODELS?

Anything glue-able—instant glue-able!

THE BEAUTY OF YOUR STARSHIP DESIGNS ARE THEIR SIMPLICITY AND ELEGANCE. WHAT INSPIRED YOU?

They had to have that kind of synergy among themselves. Another thing to draw on was World War II aircraft spotting. As kids we had these German, Italian, French, and British airplane models. Each had a gesture [special trait] by which you could tell right away what country they were from. In this case, the TIEs had to have an alien country.

HOW DOES THE TIE FIGHTER MATCH AS THE X-WING'S VILLAINOUS COUNTERPART?

The X-wing is very humanistic and, in fact, gets very close to an ordinary airplane when it's landing. The wings collapse to horizontal, and its guns go back into its holsters.

The TIE fighter had to be ominous and its weaponry mysterious. You can't even tell what part of it is shooting. It is incredibly destructive, and yet it doesn't use the same movements as the Rebel craft when launching or maneuvering for an attack. In a group, the relation of one TIE behind another one—which one's the leader—is very clearly seen. But a TIE can then suddenly depart and not be constrained in the same ways that a fighter plane would. So the TIE's whole repertoire is that it has to be a different kind of dancer.

In other words, there is a ballet between the TIE and X-wing that communicates different kinds of warriorship.

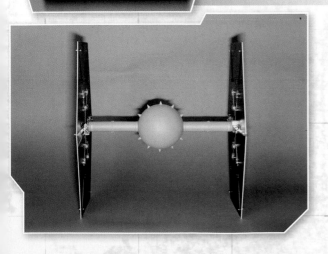

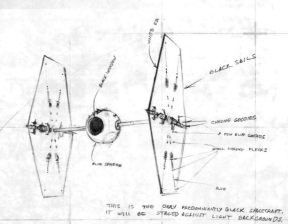

THIS IS THE ONLY PREDOMINANTLY BLACK SPACECRAFT. IT WILL BE STAGED AGAINST LIGHT BACKGROUNDS.

DRAWING BY COLIN CANTWELL

MAKE IT YOUR OWN

One of the great things about IncrediBuilds models is that each one is completely customizable. The untreated natural wood can be decorated with paints, pencils, pens, beads, sequins—the list goes on and on!

BEFORE YOU BEGIN
Read through the included instruction sheet so you understand how all the pieces come together. Then, you can make one of these projects or try something completely different!

TIE FIGHTER REPLICA

When making a replica, it's always good to study an actual image of what you are trying to copy. Look closely at details and brainstorm how you can recreate them.

WHAT YOU NEED
• Black, gray, and red paint
• Small paintbrush
• Painter's or model tape

OPTIONAL
• Detail paintbrush
  (such as 18/0 spotter)
• Small, flat bright brush

1. After assembling the model, paint the body of the TIE fighte gray. Make sure you paint in all the nooks and crannies.

2. Pick a wing to paint first and start on the outside of the win If you're using tape, you will need six pieces. Following the engraving, tape the wings so the edges are showing. Paint i the borders with gray.

3. Let the paint dry and then remove the tape slowly to get a straight line. You can touch up any mistakes with a small paintbrush.

4. Now tape off the "spokes" of the wings. Note that there are engravings that surround the "spokes." You will want to tap around those as well to get a good line. Paint the spokes an center gray. Let dry.

5. The inside of the wings are tricky because there are no engravings. Create your own lines with tape, matching clos to the outside wing. Then, follow the techniques used in ste 3 and 4.

6. After the gray is dry and the tape has been removed, paint i the black sections on the wings.

7. Repeat steps 2 through 6 on the other wing.

8. Using a very small brush, paint in the "windows" of the coc with black paint. You will need to be careful. Leave the line: gray around each section to create a good outline.

9. Finish by adding two dots of red paint to the back for engine (Not shown.)

REBEL-COMMANDEERED TIE FIGHTER

What if the Rebel Alliance captured a TIE fighter? Perhaps they would paint the Rebel Alliance insignia on the wings to make it clear that it's no longer an Imperial craft.

WHAT YOU NEED
- Black, gray, and red paint
- Small paintbrush
- Painter's or model tape

OPTIONAL
- Detail paintbrush (such as 18/0 spotter)
- Small, flat bright brush

1. Follow the Replica instructions on page 28.

2. Trace the image of the Rebel Alliance insignia on the page.

3. Cover the back of your traced image with tape.

4. Cut out the symbol. You can use either the outline left or the piece cut out as a stencil.

5. Lay stencil over the wing of the TIE fighter. Hold in place with one hand (or tape it down) and paint either inside the stencil or around it, depending on how you made your stencil. If you create a line around the stencil, pull off the stencil and fill in the outline.

RACING TIE FIGHTER

Who would win in a race—a TIE fighter or an X-wing? It certainly would help the TIE fighter to have some snazzy racing stripes and cool checkered-flag wings.

WHAT YOU NEED
- Black, white, and red paint
- Small paintbrush
- Sharp pencil
- Straight edge

OPTIONAL
- Glossy black paint
- White and black paint pens
- Detail paintbrush (such as 18/0 spotter)
- Small, flat bright brush

1. To start, you need to work on the wings. Take pieces 42 and 45 out of the board before you start building the model. You'll need to draw a grid on both sides of each wing.

2. Using your pencil and a straight edge, draw a vertical line down the middle of the wing.

3. Next, draw a horizontal line down the middle of the wing.

4. Starting from the first vertical line, draw evenly spaced vertical lines on each side.

5. Then, from the center horizontal line, draw evenly spaced horizontal lines on each side.

6. Using paint pens or regular paints, color the grid into a checkerboard pattern.

7. Edge the wings with black paint.

8. Assemble the model.

9. Paint the "spokes" red.

10. Paint some of the edges of the model red for "racing stripes" as shown.

11. Carefully paint around the red stripes with black paint. Fill in all the nooks and crannies.

12. Paint the face of the cockpit red.

13. Using a tiny brush, fill in the windows of the cockpit with black, making sure to leave the red as an outline.

R2-D2 TIE FIGHTER

What would happen if you took a TIE fighter from the Dark Side and blended it with a lovable hero of the Rebel Alliance? Try this epic mashup of two iconic symbols from the films for a completely new look.

WHAT YOU NEED
- White, silver, blue, and black paint
- Small paintbrush
- Painter's or model tape

OPTIONAL
- Red paint
- Detail paintbrush (such as 18/0 spotter)
- Small, flat bright brush

1. For this model, you will need to paint the wings before assembling the model. Start by painting both sides of each wing white.

2. After the white is dry, follow steps 2 and 3 from the Replica project (page 28), replacing gray paint with blue.

3. Next, study the photo of R2-D2. Pick out details and shapes you would like to put on the wings.

4. Pencil in the details you want to add.

5. Paint over the pencil lines to get the shapes you want.

6. After paint is dry, assemble the model.

7. Now paint the remaining sections in order from light to dark: white, silver, blue, and black.

PAINTING TIPS
To paint the "spokes" on the wings, refer to step 3 from the Replica instructions (page 28).

For the cockpit: Paint the front white. After it dries, use a tiny brush to fill in the silver sections, then the blue sections, and then the black. Finish by adding the dot of white.

SOURCES

Astleford, Gary, Owen K.C. Stephens, and Rodney Thompson. *Starships of the Galaxy*. 2nd ed. Renton, WA: Wizards of the Coast, 2007.

Bray, Adam, Cole Horton, Kerrie Dougherty, and Michael Kogge. *Star Wars: Absolutely Everything You Need to Know*. New York: Dorling Kindersley, 2015.

Bouzereau, Laurent. *Star Wars: The Annotated Screenplays*. New York: Del Rey, 1997.

Dougherty, Kerrie, Curtis Saxton, David West Reynolds, and Ryder Windham. *Star Wars: Complete Vehicles*. New York: Dorling Kindersley, 2013.

Blackman, Haden. *The New Essential Guide to Vehicles and Vessels*. New York: Del Rey, 2003.

Gorden, Greg. *Imperial Sourcebook*. 1st ed. Honesdale, PA: West End Games, 1989.

Kogge, Michael. *Star Wars Rebels: Battle to the End*. Los Angeles: Disney-Lucasfilm Press, 2015.

Peterson, Lorne. *Sculpting a Galaxy*. San Rafael, CA: Insight Editions, 2006.

Reynolds, David West, James Luceno, and Ryder Windham. *The Complete Star Wars Visual Dictionary*. New York: Dorling Kindersley, 2006.

Rinzler, J.W. *The Making of Star Wars*. New York: Del Rey, 2007.

———. *The Sounds of Star Wars*. San Francisco: Chronicle, 2010.

———. *Star Wars: The Blueprints*. Seattle: 47North, 2013.

Slavicsek, Bill. *Death Star Technical Companion*. Honesdale, PA: West End Games, 1991.

Slavicsek, Bill and Curtis Smith. *The Star Wars Sourcebook*. Honesdale, PA: West End Games, 1987.

Smith, Bill. *The Essential Guide to Vehicles and Vessels*. New York: Del Rey, 1996.

———. *The New Essential Guide to Droids*. New York: Del Rey, 2006.

Windham, Ryder. *Star Wars: Millennium Falcon Owner's Workshop Manual*. Del Rey: New York, 2011.

Insight Editions would like to thank Curt Baker, Leland Chee, Pablo Hidalgo, Samantha Holland, Daniel Saeva, and Krista Wong.

ABOUT THE AUTHOR

MICHAEL KOGGE'S other recent work includes *Empire of the Wolf*, an epic graphic novel featuring werewolves in ancient Rome, and the *Star Wars Rebels* series of books. He resides online at www.MichaelKogge.com, while his real home is in Los Angeles.

IncrediBuilds™
A Division of Insight Editions LP
PO Box 3088
San Rafael, CA 94912
www.insighteditions.com

Find us on Facebook: www.facebook.com/InsightEditions
Follow us on Twitter: @insighteditions

© & ™ 2016 LUCASFILM LTD. Used Under Authorization.

Published by Insight Editions, San Rafael, California, in 2016. No part of this book may be reproduced in any form without written permission from the publisher.

Library of Congress Cataloging-in-Publication Data available.

ISBN: 978-1-68298-004-0

Publisher: Raoul Goff
Art Director: Chrissy Kwasnik
Designer: Ashley Quackenbush
Executive Editor: Vanessa Lopez
Senior Editor: Chris Prince
Production Editor: Elaine Ou
Editorial Assistant: Katie DeSandro
Production Manager: Anna Wan
Craft and Instruction Development: Rebekah Piatte
Craft Photography: Anthony Piatte

ROOTS of PEACE · REPLANTED PAPER

Insight Editions, in association with Roots of Peace, will plant two trees for each tree used in the manufacturing of this book. Roots of Peace is an internationally renowned humanitarian organization dedicated to eradicating land mines worldwide and converting war-torn lands into productive farms and wildlife habitats. Roots of Peace will plant two million fruit and nut trees in Afghanistan and provide farmers there with the skills and support necessary for sustainable land use.

Manufactured in China by Insight Editions

10 9 8 7 6 5 4 3 2 1